INGRES

PIERRE GAUDIBERT

GROSSET & DUNLAP
Publishers - New York

First American edition published by Grosset & Dunlap, Inc.
All rights reserved
Translated from the Italian by Diane Goldrei
Translation copyright © 1971 by Thames and Hudson, London
Copyright © 1969 by Sadea Editore, Firenze
Library of Congress Catalog Card Number: 78-122024

Printed and bound in Italy

Life and works

The work of Ingres abounds in contradictions. It aroused controversy during his lifetime and continues to do so today. The eccentricities of his art reflect the quirks of his own personality. His work suggests that he never strayed from rigidly held principles, and yet the *Self-portrait at the age of twenty-four (pl. 1)* reveals a passionate young man. With his admission to the Académie des Beaux-Arts, his work became identified as the epitome of classicism, but in earlier years contemporaries had found a violent romanticism and neo-Gothic mannerisms in some of his paintings. Although Ingres's innovations still continued to be highly controversial, he came to acquire an aura of classicism.

Jean-Auguste-Dominique Ingres was born in Montauban on 29 August 1780. A few years later, the whole of Europe was shaken by the French Revolution. But neither this upheaval nor its political consequences, which affected the course of his own life, could shake his aesthetic convictions or his determination to follow his chosen path, the search for Beauty. If the Romantics, with their extreme sensibility, were the heirs of the French Revolution, Ingres was not one of them. He had the indifference of a provincial to the political temper of the times.

His father, Jean-Marie-Joseph Ingres, was architect, painter, sculptor and musician, one of those unassuming jacks-of-all-trades who survived in the French provinces until the end of the eighteenth century. Ingres learned the rudiments of draughtsmanship and music from his father. From the age of eleven to sixteen, Ingres studied in Toulouse, where he was a pupil of the sculptor Jean-Pierre Vigan and of Joseph Roques, who had been a disciple of the eighteenth-century neoclassicist Vien. Jean Briant taught Ingres the art of landscape painting. Ingres's love for Raphael is supposed to date from this period, when he is said to have seen a copy, made by Roques in Florence, of Raphael's *Madonna of the Chair*. A talented violinist, Ingres played

3

in the orchestra of the Toulouse theatre every evening. He was a fervent admirer of Gluck.

In 1796, with an introduction from his teachers, Ingres arrived in Paris and joined the school of David, then the undisputed master of the arts. Aspiring artists, hoping to make an international name for themselves, flocked to his school. It was here that Ingres met his future friend, the Italian sculptor Bartolini, who was to take him to Florence. David's school was a thriving centre for the elaboration of theory of the figurative arts. David's pupils divided into two major groups: the *Penseurs* or *Primitifs* and the *Muscadins*. The *Primitifs* preached a return to the archaic style. They held that, after Phidias, Greek art had been led astray by the search for theatrical effects, and had degenerated into mannerism. In keeping with their desire for pure solemnity, they favoured a return to ancient themes: the Bible, Homer and Ossian, the epic poems, which they regarded as the only valid source of inspiration. The Catholic and monarchist *Muscadins* were interested in the Middle Ages, and Alexandre Lenoir's Musée des Monuments Français. Ingres did not belong to either group; from this time on, his eclecticism was his outstanding characteristic. As a young man, and in later years, he developed the themes of the *Primitifs*, and adopted their formal archaism, but at the same time he was drawn to the troubadour subjects of the *Muscadins*. Above all he was a diligent student. He copied David's *Oath of the Horatii*, and on the strength of this David chose him as his assistant for the portrait of Madame Récamier, in which Ingres painted some minor additions.

In 1799, Ingres entered the Ecole des Beaux-Arts. He won second place in the Grand Prix de Rome in 1800, and the first prize in the following year. This entitled him to study for four years at the French Academy in Rome. His prize-winning work was an ambitious history painting, *The Envoys to Agamemnon*, in which the envoys of Agamemnon and the Greek princes, preceded by heralds, enter Achilles' tent to urge him to fight. This is the work of a brilliant young artist of the neoclassical school. Many authors have shown how Ingres found his source material in statues, rather than in the Greek vases to which he was to turn for inspiration in later years. The fragmentary nature of the composition might be put down to the inexperience of youth, but it was a weakness which was to recur in all his large canvases. The sensitivity of Ingres's line is already present in the interlacing of the figures of Achilles and Patrocles.

From 1801 to 1806, when Ingres finally left for Rome, after delays caused by political events, he lived with a group of about twenty artists, including Gros, Girodet, Granet and Bartolini, in the old Capuchin monastery in Paris, which had been turned into an artistic community. Ingres earned his living by illustrating books, and with his drawings – rapid pencil-drawn sketches of his subjects. His reputation as a portrait painter received the ultimate accolade when in 1803 a portrait of *Napoleon as First Consul* was commissioned for the city of Liège, and in 1806 he painted his *Napoleon I on the Imperial Throne*. The monumental figure seen frontally, together with the minute decorative detail, especially the eagle motif of the carpet, make this a strange, almost baroque work. It is influenced by the sumptuous traditions of the seventeenth century, and indeed it may be this which gives it such a baroque quality. Ingres was hailed as a revolutionary for this work in the Salon of 1806, before his departure for Rome.

The drawing of the *Forestier family* also dates from this year. Ingres was engaged to the daughter, who was inconsolable when her engagement to Monsieur Ingres came to an end. Ingres's first drawings already reveal his mastery of the art of portraiture, which was fully established with his paintings of the Rivière family (*pls 2-5*) and of *Mme Aymon,* known as *La Belle Zélie (pls 6-7).* Ingres was to perfect his art, but essentially it remained unchanged. His subsequent development, and even his Italian experiences, only confirmed it.

From 1806 to 1810, Ingres lived at the French Academy, the Villa Medici, in Rome. He discovered the collections in the Vatican, and the Sistine Chapel. He painted his *Oedipus and the Sphinx (pls 17-18)* and the *Jupiter and Thetis (pl. 23).* The *Bathing Woman (pls 19-20)*, known as the *Bather of Valpinçon*, marks the first appearance of the female nude in Ingres's work. It was to be the recurring theme of his career, culminating in *The Turkish Bath (pls 75-78)*. Italy became his cultural homeland, as it had been for Claude Lorrain and Poussin. ('I belong to my country, I am a Gaul, but not of those who sacked Rome, and wished to burn Delphi.') After leaving the French Academy, he settled in Rome and remained there until 1820.

In 1810, Rome came under French control. Ingres painted *Romulus, conqueror of Acron (pls 25-27)*, and *The Dream of Ossian (pl. 28)* for the imperial palace of Montecavallo, and *Virgil reading from the Aeneid before Augustus and Livia* for the Villa Aldobrandini, residence of the governor of Rome. He painted portraits of important French officials and their wives, and supplemented his income with countless drawings. He sent regular entries to the Salon. In 1813 he married Madeleine Chapelle, after he had asked for her hand on the strength of a portrait. It was to be an untroubled marriage; she was his faithful companion in difficult times, and watched as zealously over her husband's artistic integrity as he did himself. She died in 1849. In 1852 he married Delphine Ramel. He had no other love affairs. His life was completely bound up with his career as a painter, 'this sincere love of art which no one can deny me'. He always longed for a peaceful life which would enable him to slowly bring to completion the work for which he was to be remembered by posterity.

Ingres continued to be unaffected by political events. In 1814 he painted the *Recumbent Odalisque (pls 29-32)*, known as the *Grande Odalisque*, in 1830 the *Martyrdom of St Symphorian (pls 53-54)*, and in 1848 the *Venus Anadyomene (p. 29)*. His work was a startling contrast to that of his teacher, David, and of Géricault, the 'apostle of ugliness', whose *Raft of the Medusa* appeared in the Salon of 1819. The only events in Italy which interested him were the papal ceremonies with their lavish pomp and grandiose Renaissance settings. In the Sistine Chapel, Ingres copied the frescoes of Michelangelo, Botticelli and Pinturicchio. He was perhaps one of the last great painters to believe that one had only to study the old masters, while standing aloof from the course of history, to attain their beauty. But history

Lucien Bonaparte, 1807-08. 23.6×18.5 cm. New York, Goelet collection.

has not spared Ingres, and his indifference to social and political reality is undoubtedly a factor in the passing from fashion of Ingres's *grand genre*.

He was an assiduous student of the old masters. In 1820, while staying with Bartolini in Florence, he saw the Brancacci chapel in the Carmine church for the first time. He loved Raphael, and the masters who preceded him; he liked Cimabue, Giotto and their followers, and Botticelli. He was one of the first to appreciate the importance of the Italian fifteenth century, the Quattrocento, in the history of art. He admired Andrea del Sarto and the seventeenth-century French artists who, like him, had been strongly influenced by Italian art. Thus, we can see the influence of Poussin in the figure in the background of *Oedipus and the Sphinx* (*pls 17-18*). He liked Lesueur, who so exaggerated Raphael's sweetness, and Philippe de Champaigne with his austere figurative mysticism. He discovered the importance of line in the Etruscan vases and Greek bas-reliefs which were to inspire his figures: the profiles in *Jupiter and Thetis*, and *Oedipus and the Sphinx*, for example, and even his portraits of Desdéban (*pl. 22*) and Madame Cavé. 'It is through contact with the creations of others that we ourselves learn to create'. This classical credo, which underlies Ingres's frequently all-too-obvious eclecticism, was to be held against him by those who favoured innovation rather than classicism in art.

When Ingres arrived in Florence in 1820, France had lost control over Italy, and as a result, Ingres had lost his clientele. This was a period of financial difficulty (he had increasingly to turn to drawing to make a living) and of lack of success at the Paris Salon, where his audacity and 'Gothic' taste came under fire. During this period he painted *Roger and Angelica* (*pls 35-38*), in 1819, and the *Entry of Charles V into Paris* in 1821, both in the so-called 'troubadour' genre, and from 1821 to 1824 he was working on the *Vow of Louis XIII* (*pls 43-44*). His success in the Salon of 1824, where Delacroix exhibited the *Massacre of Scio*, came too late. Ingres was now forty-four years old. His future rival, Delacroix, had already emerged in 1822 at the age of twenty-four as the leader of a school, with his painting of *Dante's Bark*. Flushed with success, Ingres returned to France, where he received the Croix de la Légion d'Honneur and was elected a member of the Académie des Beaux-Arts. He opened a studio in what is now the Rue Visconti. With the death of David, and after the suicide of Gros in 1835, Ingres became the acknowledged leader of the classical school, the champion of 'beautiful painting' (*la belle peinture*). It is ironic to recall how Ingres, with his love of local colour, and under attack from the academic artists, had once been the darling of the future Romantics.

From 1827 to 1834, Théodore Chassériau and several future pupils of the Villa Medici – Amaury-Duval, Hippolyte Flandrin, and Lehmann – came to his studio. In 1826-27, Ingres was working on his *Apotheosis of Homer* for the ceiling of the Egyptian and Etruscan room in the Musée Charles X, now the Musée du Louvre. Ingres's picture is a paean to poetic art: all those who have contributed to the advance of human thought are assembled in a Pantheon of illustrious men who pay homage to the greatest of them all. In 1840, Ingres was to return to this theme with his drawing of the *Deification of Homer*, in which the absence of Shakespeare and Tasso is symptomatic of the increased rigidity of his ideas. On his return to France he had also begun work on the *Martyrdom of St Symphorian* (*pls 53-54*), which was supposed to be his definitive artistic statement. Ingres put an enormous amount of work into this painting. There are two hundred studies for it in the museum in Montauban. The *Martyrdom of St Symphorian* was exhibited at the Salon in 1834 and was unfavourably received by nearly all the critics. Ingres's disappointment was such that he closed his studio and decided to stop exhibiting at the Salon. The only occasion on which he later relented was the Exposition Universelle of 1855. He refused all official commissions, and finally, to escape from Paris, requested and was granted the post of director of the French Academy in Rome.

From 1835 to 1841, Ingres, an exile of mounting prestige, was the highly active director of the Villa Medici, where his former pupils had reassembled. He introduced an archaeology course and set up a library. The worldly atmosphere which had prevailed under his predecessor, Horace Verne, gave way to the somewhat melancholy austerity of a man who had chosen to relinquish everything for art, even his natural predilection for women. The bulk of his time was taken up with administering the Academy, and he produced little work of his own. He painted three pictures in six years: the first version of *Antiochus and Stratonice*, the *Odalisque with Slave (pls 62-65)*, and *Raphael and the Fornarina (pls 55-56)*.

After his triumphal return to Paris in 1841, from 1843 to 1849 Ingres applied himself to the decoration of the gallery in the Château de Dampierre with the theme, the *Golden Age*, which was never completed, and the *Iron Age*, of which only an outline was made. He prepared the cartoons for the windows of the chapel of St Ferdinand at Neuilly and for the chapel of St Louis, commissioned by the Orléans royal family. From this time on, a halo of legend began to surround the figure of Ingres, and his eccentricities became public property.

During the Second Republic, he was nominated as a member of the Permanent Commission of Fine Arts. Before resigning his membership in May 1849, he had given his full support to the proposal to abolish the jury system and institute complete freedom of admission to the Salon. The Exposition Universelle of 1855 included more than sixty of his works, and in the same year he was nominated a Grand Officer of the Legion of Honour. In 1862 he completed *The Turkish Bath (pls 75-78)*. Napoleon III conferred the title of Senator on him, and appointed him a member of the Imperial Council of Public Instruction.

While Ingres's art ossified under the weight of these official honours, a new generation of artists fought the battles in which he had once been in the vanguard. In 1851, Gustave Courbet exhibited his *Burial at Ornans*, and in 1863, the jury of the Salon rejected Manet's *Déjeuner sur l'Herbe*. Some of these painters, among them Degas, for example, who were to revolutionize art, were influenced by Ingres both in their drawing and their painting. Ingres died in 1867. His last work was a drawing of Giotto's *Christ at the Tomb*.

Ingres was the last traditional artist to remain true to the inheritance of the seventeenth century. Like his predecessors, he was a firm believer in the traditional hierarchy of the genres. His guiding principle was imitation; more precisely, he wanted to recreate the achievements of ancient Greece. 'Everything has been done before, everything has already been invented. Our task is not to invent, but to continue what has already been achieved.' He echoes Boileau in his belief in the search for perfection, rather than in an inventive art. He returns to the same themes in his quest for the absolute form worthy of an absolute and eternal aesthetic. He painted *Oedipus and the Sphinx* in 1808 and 1864; *Virgil reading from the Aeneid* in 1808 and 1811. There are five versions of *Paolo and Francesca*, three of *Roger and Angelica*, four of *Raphael and the Fornarina*, and a whole series of *Odalisques* which recur throughout his career. Baudelaire said of Ingres: 'He is a man who has built himself a system', and who had only one passion, the passion for style. This striving after perfection was the justification for the almost obsessive recurrence of his themes.

Ingres wanted to be 'a painter of history, and not a portrait painter of the bourgeoisie'. Hence his concentration on heroic subjects, in which this aim is manifest: the *Vow of Louis XIII*, the *Apotheosis of Homer*, the *Martyrdom of St Symphorian*. He aimed at an epic scale, hence his monumentality. In his early works, *Napoleon I on the Imperial Throne, Oedipus and the Sphinx (pls 17-18), Jupiter and Thetis (pl. 23)*, he seeks to achieve this epic quality by allowing one figure, in the frontal view, to dominate the canvas space, to the exclusion of all else. In *Joan of Arc at the Coronation of Charles VII (pl. 68)*, 1854, his main figure is again disproportionately large. Ingres often has recourse to this device in his compositions, and particularly in the more complex ones, in which the central figures are painted full face (the figure of Homer in the *Apotheosis*, the Virgin in *The Vow of Louis XIII (pls 43-44)*, St Symphorian (*pls 53-54*), or the figure of Christ in *Jesus among the Doctors (pls 80-82)*, he remains tied to the frontal view. This explains the rigidity of the compositions, in which the subtlety of the line cannot disguise the essential structure, based on a central axis.

In the works where the central figure does not occupy the whole space of the canvas, the composition is built in a pyramid shape (as in the *Apotheosis of Homer* or *Jesus among the Doctors*) which fixes the figures, without giving the scene depth. The scene seems to be artificially widened and frozen in austere geometric symmetry. Sometimes the composition is divided into two levels, as in the *Vow of Louis XIII* and the *Martyrdom of St Symphorian*, giving the work a heterogeneous appearance, in which Ingres's eclecticism is at its most marked. This split renders the canvas lifeless. Ingres cannot handle compositions which are based on movement alone.

The immobility of Ingres's compositions is heightened by the stilted gestures of his figures: we have only to look at the gestures of Romulus or St Sebastian, which seem quite unrelated to the tumult around them. In the work of David, vigorous design and a Roman spirit enliven the uncompromisingly forceful *Oath of the Horatii*; Delacroix looked to Rubens and the other baroque artists for the secret of ' spectacular ' art, which lies in compositions based on diagonal lines, circular movement and the interplay of colour. All this is absent from the work of Ingres. The gestures of his figures are meaningless and academic. The expressions of his Virgins and his Joan of Arc *(pl. 68)* are merely theatrical stereotypes of humility and benevolence. Their eyes modestly cast down, or raised to heaven, they are actresses playing the part of pious women.

Although Ingres was a believer in the purity of painting, his historical paintings are literary. Unable to convey a sense of drama, he has to express drama through symbols. In *Oedipus and the Sphinx, (pls 17-18)*, for example, the glowering stare of the Sphinx, and the figure in the background whose isolation is heightened by the crevice in the cave, are supposed to add to the sense of terror. The foot of a corpse and the skeleton, together with the exaggerated chiaroscuro, underline the message already repeated *ad nauseam*.

Look at the figure of Juno, the eagle and the bas-relief in *Jupiter and Thetis (pl. 23)*. All that is lacking is Jupiter's thunderbolt, although the menacing clouds suggest that even this was not far from the artist's mind. The composition is crammed with literary devices. The same applies to *Cherubini and the Muse of Lyric Poetry (pls 59-60)*. The portrait of Cherubini is very fine, but Ingres was unable to express all aspects of the personality in it, and he resorts to allegory to express Cherubini's musical genius.

Ingres is not at his best with myths. His slow, painstaking search for perfection diminishes the grandeur of his subjects. His preoccupation with detail is like that of a miniaturist; Delacroix was not far off the mark when he called the *Apotheosis of Homer* an 'enlarged cameo.' To what must we attribute Ingres's failure with mythical subjects? Perhaps we should hold his eclecticism responsible; and yet there are few identifiable sources for the equally unsuccessful *Martyrdom of St Symphorian*. In fact his need to refer to other artists is no more than a symptom of his lack of any real feeling for this type of painting. His contemporaries, including Stendhal, noted his lack of religious feeling. Baudelaire criticized him for being impervious to the supernatural, for failing to look beyond appearances for a mystical quality.

Ingres's interest lay only in what he saw: he was fascinated by appearances. This man, who stood aloof from history, from politics, from his own times, indeed from time itself, lacked any sense of drama. There is no contact between the figures in his canvases: they do not look at each other, hence the absurd incompleteness of their gestures, which seem to bear no real relation to the rest of the picture. The figures seem to be grouped together to form a monolithic whole, like *Paolo and Francesca (pl. 39)* linked only by their kiss, or else they mingle in a featureless throng, as in *The Turkish Bath (pls 75-78)*. This is the only kind of interplay of figures in Ingres's work; its effect is sensual rather than dramatic. It can have no place in historical works. There is a temptation to dismiss Ingres's historical paintings outright. But this is unjustifiable in a work of criticism. Succeeding generations may of course prefer some aspects of an artist's works to others, but the choice must be made against the background of his achievement in its entirety. The female form, the central theme in Ingres's work, appears in his historical painting just as it does elsewhere. *Jupiter and Thetis (pl. 23)*, was much ridiculed by critics, who said that Thetis, with her elongated neck, appeared to be suffering from a goitre; her body describes an arc, which emphasizes the mannered drapery encasing her. She has the sensual face, the solemn, fixed gaze, of the *Odalisques*. The strange *Dream of Ossian (pl. 28)* is a characteristic work. Commissioned in 1811 and painted between 1812 and 1813, Ingres later returned to it, but never completed it. In this painting idealized but undramatic figures emerge from the ghostlike pallor cast by a light, which is most unusual in Ingres's work. But it is symptomatic of Ingres that this light does not serve to dramatize the scene, but to emphasize its unreality. Ingres was able to describe visions, insubstantial images, figures lost in an evanescent throng, with a total absence of drama. In this Valhalla of the warriors, the only beings who have real physical substance are the female figures, their sensual, melodious lines petrified in the idyllic vision. The *Golden Age*, an unfinished work, is also an epic tribute to the female human body. This composition succeeds because the figures are linked in the rhythm and the embrace of the dance, in a sensual rite, a pagan cult of the body, which has nothing to do with history and man's place in history.

These mannered, miniature-like images have a strange appeal, which is also to be found in Ingres's paintings of medieval subjects. His *St Adelaide (pl. 58)*, for example, one of the cartoons for the chapel of St Ferdinand, has the sinuous refinement of a Gothic statue. The colours are the ' marvellous colours of the icon, of miniatures'. The rules of perspective are turned upside down: the glowing colours of the background, and particularly the yellows, bring the rear planes forward, as in *Jesus among the Doctors*. On other occasions, he ignores the rules altogether and applies a uniform use of colour: flat shades which bring the background and the figures on to the same plane, as in his cartoons for the windows of St Ferdinand. The fullness of the forms bound by a sharp line, in the cartoon of *Charity*, for example, gives them a decorative quality comparable to that of Fernand Léger, who made deliberate use of the play of colour in giving depth or greater emphasis, to enhance or contrast with architectural volumes. Ingres was one of the first artists to use colour in order to dispense with the third dimension.

Colour destroys perspective and enhances plasticity; this may be the reason for his failure as an historical painter. Historical painting, in so far as it is dramatic and an account of deeds, has much in common with the theatre. The canvas becomes a kind of Italian stage: the cube of the Renaissance perspective view. Ingres's painting ignores the third dimension; when he wants to suggest depth, as in the *Martyrdom of St Symphorian* (*pls 53-54*) the background is lost in an indistinct mist which closes the composition instead of opening it up. This peculiarity, the underlying reason for Ingres's failure in the heroic style, was at the same time an important contribution to the breach with Renaissance tradition which was to be completed only in the twentieth century, and which consisted in bringing the images back to the surface.

The classical theory of imitation expected the artist, following in the footsteps of the old masters, to base himself on nature, purifying it through the nobility of his stylistic interpretation. This doctrine serves to define the realism of Ingres's Italian landscapes and his portraits, which are his masterpieces. Ingres's realism, like all his art, contains an element of ambiguity.

From early childhood he noted down his surroundings in his sketches, a habit that must have been encouraged by his family, who were astounded by his precocious talent. Towards the end of his life, Ingres estimated that he had drawn about 300 pencil portraits, and we know of 450 such drawings today. In the difficult years in Italy, after 1815, he earned his living by his drawings, which were sold to tourists, especially English tourists. When success freed him from financial worries after 1824, he forgot his aversion to this commercial art form and began to draw for his friends. These drawings were unknown to his contemporaries, and about fifty of them were shown for the first time in 1861, to an enthusiastic public at the Salon des Arts-Unis.

Today, these drawings have an outstanding reputation; they rank Ingres with Holbein and the French draughtsmen of the sixteenth century. He has given us a picture of a true *Comédie Humaine*. Technically, the drawings are highly interesting, since they were very rapidly executed, unlike his paintings which were the result of a slow, deliberate process. They took three or four hours, and Ingres tried only one or two poses at most. He often sketched his subjects as they were, at the dinner table. Ingres shows great spontaneity in these drawings, an ability to capture the vitality of a pose or expression. They have a ' contained ' truth, to borrow Hans Naef's phrase, a psychological insight, which is all the more remarkable in one so utterly devoid of psychological understanding as Ingres. Perhaps this achievement was possible because of the artist's direct, immediate approach, which enabled him to capture a revealing pose or expression without second thoughts.

Ingres's drawings are very varied in style. Some are very free and economical, especially those for his friends, for example the drawing of *Mme Hittorf*, in which the eyes, the hair and the roundness of the face are drawn with great delicacy and precision, while the pose and the dress are sketched in with rapid strokes. This subtle contrast in style gives the drawing a refined, poetic quality, as if the graceful face were emerging from the flowing softness of silk. There is only a hint of the unrestrained preciosity of Ingres's painted portraits.

Some of the other drawings, particularly those which were commissioned, are more polished. Their precision is extraordinary. Ingres's sensitivity still has the meticulous refinement of classicism. In the portrait of *Mme Guillon-Lethière and her son Lucien* the jewels, the trimmings, the curls in her hair, are rendered with great care. In the background, the Roman landscape fades into the distance, not through the softness of the shading, but through the gradually decreasing precision of the detail.

This is also true of the rather paradoxical landscape sketches which the artist made during his stay in Rome. The fore-

Monsieur A. Lethière, 1815. Collection Bonnat.

ground is virtually empty, as in the *View of Tivoli* (*pl. 21*), or sketched in with swift and abstract strokes, as in the *View of the Villa Medici* (*pls 8-9*), while the background is drawn with precision. This technique is not merely artistic prowess. It is a departure from traditional methods of representation. Ingres's drawings are at least as daringly novel as the ' medieval' or ' Gothic' paintings, which aroused a storm of controversy. Ingres, who was grappling with the renewed problem of perspective, reaches a creative peak in his drawings. Here again, we can now see how far his work and stylistic experiments contributed towards the elimination of the vanishing point and the figurative rhetoric inherited from the sixteenth century. He was indeed, essentially an observer, an artist who recorded what he saw. His visual clarity is that of the Impressionists, who were to go so far as to doubt the validity both of traditional painting and of observation.

In Italy, Ingres painted three landscapes (*pls 8-13*); they were to be his last. They are painted on wood, and this, together with their circular form, which has the illusive effect of an open window, and their small size (about six inches in diameter), turns them into miniatures. These works, particularly *The Casino of Raphael in Rome* (*pls 12-13*), are very closely related to the drawings. The composition, with the empty foreground and the carefully detailed background, is very similar. The landscape is always described at the back of the picture, as in Italian Renaissance paintings. The design picks out each feature in turn, illuminated by the clarity of the local colour, which neither the atmosphere nor the still light can impair. ' Light is like water ... it immediately finds its own level.'

This level is that of a calm mid-day, at its purest when all the colours of the spectrum are absorbed in the intensely bright, almost grey light. ' The colours must not be too warm .... Exaggerate the greys rather than the warm colours, if you wish to paint well.' Subtle colour, the colour Ingres admires in Titian, is ' true colour,' that is, local colour. ' The essential part of the colouring is not the effect of the light and dark masses in the painting, but the particular distinctive tone of each object.' The light from the sun at its zenith annihilates shadow, and objects are revealed as they really are, ' buried in their form ' as Gaetan Picon says, with no other mystery than that of excessive luminosity, an intellectual, analytic luminosity. In his landscape paintings Ingres is a classical artist, far removed from the course the Impressionists were to take.

The unwavering light is surprisingly limpid, as if the sun had purified the atmosphere. And indeed, in Mediterranean countries the light does very often have this quality. Ingres's ability to capture the transparency of air anticipates the Italian followers of Corot. The fine gradations of feeling in these miniatures, together with Ingres's intellectual discernment, give them a subtle poetic quality. Ingres's realism dominates this delicate composition, in which he observes and lovingly notes down the tangible world. There is no trace of the human form. The only human figure in *The Casino of Raphael in Rome* is a statue. Nature, like painting, is seen as the source of a purely visual pleasure.

As a portrait painter, Ingres remained loyal to the teachings of David until 1806. In his portraits of Desdéban (*pl. 22*) and Bartolini, the sitters, caught in mid-movement, are in a three-quarters position, against a brown background brought out by glazing. Ingres was heir to the traditions of the French portraiture of the eighteenth century, to such artists as Peyronneau, La Tour, Fragonard and David himself, whose realism demanded that the artist capture a fleeting expression, the spontaneity of life, the transitory aspects of an individual, rather than the whole personality. The drawings spring from this same realism. Ingres was to return to it in a few very rare portraits in later life, which were either very rapid portraits (Mlle Gonin) or simply sketches (M. Cavé). In other works his realism was to take a different form.

He saw the swift sketch as the basis of his earlier portraits, although there is a trace of Florentine influence in his portrait of Gilibert, in the fleeting expression, the highlights on the face, shirt and hands, which lighten the canvas, in the elegance of the linear style. Ingres considered this a finished work, even though the background and the suit are barely sketched in. He was trying here to achieve the brilliance and fineness of touch of David's drawing, and his light impasto.

The three portraits of the Rivière family (*pls 2-5*) in 1805, the masterpieces of the Parisian period which preceded his journey to Rome, mark his departure from the style of David. *M. Rivière* has been compared to David's portrait of M. Sérizat. With this portrait, Ingres brings the teachings of David to a peak of perfection. The refined luxury of the setting, which discreetly and harmoniously identifies the sitter's intellectual and social standing, while leaving the admirable structure of the figure and his easy pose intact, has all the purity of a David. It is a remarkable farewell work. The portraits of *Mme Rivière, Mlle Rivière* and *Mme Aymon* are pure, unadulterated Ingres, equal to the works of his maturity. Ingres had now discovered his own style.

Mme Aymon, known as *La Belle Zélie (pls 6-7)*, is the first of a series of monumental portraits in which a pyramidal structure dominates the canvas. In this portrait, the geometric outline of the head and the curvilinear purity of the curls, the ears and the earrings, counteract the irregularity of the model's features, particularly the rather doubtful chin which caused Ingres's knowledge of anatomy to be called in question.

Mme Rivière (pl. 3) is the first of a series of formal portraits, which are a hymn to mature womanhood. The ample contours of the sitter stretch out the two ellipses of the body and the shawl, which intersect to form a perfect balance. (We can already see in this portrait how Ingres fuses clothes and body, so that the body becomes the ornament, and the clothes are ' the metamorphosis of the body '.) The splendid velvet has a muted sensuousness which is subtly echoed in the decorative motifs of the embroidery and the shawl. The broad, soft horizontal lines offset the tension of the two ellipses, which would otherwise upset the balance of the composition. The whole canvas is painted in harmonious light tones.

Mlle Rivière (pls 4-5) is an even more typical expression of Ingres's style. With the exotic curve of nose and eyebrow, the heavy-lidded eyes, the prominent cheekbones, she has the ambiguity of adolescence, and indeed, of all Ingres's later paintings of women: a frank gaze and sensual lips, the virginal white dress, and the fur coiling sensuously round her gloved arms. The limpid landscape of the Ile de France reflects the naive and sensual placidity of the model.

The introduction of landscape into his portraits is an obvious sign of Ingres's break away from David. Ingres seems to be following Gros and Gérard in a pre-Romantic attempt to capture on canvas the secret communion between man and nature, the harmony in which ' landscape becomes a mood '. This kind of romanticism is present in the glowering skies which form the background to his *François-Marius Granet (pl. 14)* and *Count Gouriev (pl. 42)*, painted in Rome between 1807 and 1814, and *M. Cordier* (1811, *pl. 24*). However, with the exception of *Mlle Rivière*, the landscape is not lyrically in tune with the sitter. There is no fusion, no interplay between the figure and nature, and no real landscape, as there is in *Josephine at Malmaison*, for example. The landscape does not act as a metaphor.

The relationship between man and nature is essentially an emotional, almost a religious one; and Ingres has no sense of the universal. He does not probe beyond appearances. Portrait and landscape are two distinct elements arbitrarily brought together, and this conjunction gives the composition an aura of portentous solemnity. Ingres is not aiming at harmony, but at contrast, and paradox. His landscape is really the background of a miniature, and serves to project his linearly constructed subject into the foreground. He is ' Gothic ' rather than Romantic, and is closer to Renaissance traditions than to Prud'hon.

Ingres uses a monumental scale in his historical paintings in order to make the groupings more dramatic; in the portraits it serves to give his subject grandeur. The entire canvas is taken up and dominated by the monolithic mass of the sitter. This style, which is a form of hyperbole, contains a latent expressionism; it underlies the distortions that appear in some of Ingres's work. M. Bertin's hands, for example (*pl. 52*), are enlarged to support the pyramidal bulk of his body. He is distorted rather like a photograph taken with a wide-angle lens. Certain parts of his body, at the base of the picture, such as the hands, appear closer to the observer than the rest of his body. The effect is bold and startling.

The distortion and massiveness stem from the drawings. In the preparatory drawings, we see how carefully Ingres searches for the pose. He draws M. Bertin standing before he finds the dominating seated position he finally used. Ingres changed the Comtesse de Haussonville's pose several times and there are four versions of *Mme Moitessier (pls 71-72)*, on which he worked for twelve years. Ingres simplifies the design, not by 'freeing' the given elements of the human body, as he claimed, but externally, by reinforcing the outline. This gives the drawing the abstract quality, and the portrait the geometric structure, which largely contribute to the monumental impact of the composition.

Ingres sometimes adopts this enlarged design from antique art, even in his portraits. The inspiration for *Mme Moitessier* is a figure in a Pompeian painting, probably the *Pomona*. The pose of the *Comtesse de Haussonville (p. 23)* one of Ingres's favourite poses, is drawn from antique allegorical portrayals of Modesty. The sharp geometry of the drawing endows these society women with the majesty of some of his own allegories in the heroic genre: the *Odyssey (pl. 48)*, and *Charity (pl. 57)*, for example.

In his male portraits, Ingres derives his sense of monumentality from Holbein. ('Only Raphael excels him as a draughtsman.') The influence of Holbein is most noticeable in the portraits of *Frédéric Desmarais* and *Dr Defrance*. It also appears in more modified form in *M. Bertin*, and plays a part in its success. This northern element in Ingres's genius was often swamped by his Latin temperament. But there is a certain Dutch quality about the portrait of *Jeanne Gonin*, with her Calvinist austerity, in the treatment of the white satin and the delicate freshness of her white lace collar.

These monumental portraits really do conform to types. Ingres's portrait of M. Bertin, the editor of the newspaper *Le Journal des Débats*, is practically an allegory of the

La Comtesse de Haussonville, 1845. Oil on canvas, 136×92 cm. New York, Fick collection.

intellectual bourgeoisie at the time of Louis-Philippe. The Junoesque Mme Moitessier becomes the hieratic symbol of the rich bourgeoisie of the second French Empire; the opulence of her geometric forms was to inspire Picasso on at least two occasions.

Thus in the mid-nineteenth century, Ingres was the heir to the formal portrait painters of the seventeenth century. He portrays his subjects, like Pastoret and Louis Ferdinand, in the splendour of their social finery. In his female portraits luxury becomes a hymn to the femininity of his subjects. *Mme Moitessier (pls 71-72)* has the idealized but blank face of a statue. *Mme de Senonnes (pl. 33)* has an unremarkable expression, and it is, paradoxically, her profile, reflected in the mirror, hair drawn back like that of the odalisques, which has the ephemeral glow of life, and the trace of a smile. In the portrait of Mme de Senonnes, only the velvet, the satin, the voile, the cold splendour of the jewels seem to vibrate with life. The folds of the materials are so perfect that no one could possibly dare to ruffle their soft curves. Mme de Senonnes is arranged in her lush setting, like a jewel in a jewel-box, there only for us to gaze upon. She has become an object, imprisoned in the sensual magnificence surrounding her, which metaphorically expresses her femininity, just as sacred images are made to incarnate the divinity for which tributes are made to them. Her surroundings are the symbols of the cult of womanhood, and they seem to remove her from her own individual life and irradiate her with the empty splendour of idols. Mme de Senonnes is a profane icon. This is Ingres's true religion: a pagan rite which culminates in pure visual enjoyment. His imagination unfolds in a paean to ornamentation which becomes ever farther removed from reality and larger than life itself.

Life in these portraits is made up of reflections. The light dances on the mirrors, the folds of the silk, clings to the transparent voiles, the still brightness of jewels, and nestles in the opaque velvet. This light without a source spreads out in closed circles from these points of contact. The whole picture is like a reflected image, a closed and unreal world.

Whether we stress their allegorical nature or their impressive settings, these portraits are above all great hymns to human life. The starting-point of this purely visual artist's imagination is always reality, and he transforms appearances through pictorial illusion.

In the shortcomings of Ingres's historical painting, we can find the latent signs of his imaginative talent for another genre. He is neither an epic nor a political artist: but he is on surer ground with the anecdotal genre. Influenced by European 'Gothic' or medievalizing painting, encouraged in Rome by the German Nazarenes, Ingres, with his *Betrothal of Raphael*, was one of the first to introduce this genre into France. Until 1824 these 'Gothic' paintings won him the approval of the Romantics.

Even his commissioned works were successful, essentially because Ingres was able to keep to a small format, as in *King Philip V of Spain investing Marshal the Duke of Berwick with the Golden Fleece*, with its seventeenth-century crimsons. The style here is really that of miniature painting, and its charm lies in its combination of meticulousness and naivety.

When Ingres is free to choose his own subject, he is drawn to tales of love, with happy results. There is, for example, the delightful scene, in the heroic style, of *Antiochus and Stratonice (pls 83-84)*. Or *Paolo and Francesca (pl. 39)*, and *Raphael and the Fornarina (pls 55-56)*, where the figures mingle in the flowing continuity of the lines. The Fornarina, though based on Raphael's *Virgin of the Chair*, has the features and hair of the *Odalisques*. The theme really closest to Ingres's heart was woman and love.

Ingres's treatment of *Roger and Angelica (pls 35-38)* is so strange that, apart from the almost Byzantine overabundance of detail, it foreshadows the work of Gustave Moreau. The dramatic elements, the sea and the *papier mâché* monsters, are purely literary symbols. The composition seems full of a heavy silence, and the only link between the otherwise isolated figures is Roger's lance, which crosses the whole canvas. It is a love scene in which the protagonists seem oblivious of each other. The only breath of life is the arabesque curve of the woman's body, abandoned to her suffering, desirable and vulnerable (*pl. 34*).

The leitmotif of the female nude recurs throughout Ingres's career, from his earliest work through a whole series of drawings and paintings. All the bathers and odalisques reappear, assembled in what was to be to the peak of Ingres's achievement, *The Turkish Bath*, painted in 1859 at the age of seventy-nine.

The *Bathing Woman, half length, seen from behind* in the Musée Bonnat in Bayonne was painted in 1807. According to Ingres, it was the first of his studies to be inspired by the Italian old masters, and it was thus his favourite painters who suggested his most important theme. One year later, he completed the *Bather of Valpinçon* (*pls 19-20*). This woman, whose face we cannot see, reduced to the sensuous mass of her body, was to be the recurring figure in this theme, its central pivot. She reappears in the *Interior of a Harem* (*pls 49-51*), known as the *Petite Baigneuse*, which is the forerunner of *The Turkish Bath*, and *The Turkish Bath* itself (*pls 75-78*). The work recalls Bronzino, but according to Amaury-Duval, its source is an engraving of the *Coucher à l'Italienne* by Jacob Van Loo. This nude is bathed in the light found in a Vermeer, with its transparent tones and subtle harmony of cool colours. Painted in 1814, the *Grande Odalisque* (*pls 29-32*) was shown at the Salon in 1819 together with *Roger and Angelica*. Once again the critics pointed out anatomical errors. In 1811 they had called Thetis' neck the throat of a goitre sufferer. Now they found that Ingres had endowed his model with two extra vertebrae. Later they were to find fault with Angelica's neck. She was described by Henri de Waroquier as the 'woman with three breasts.' 'The third breast is where her neck should be. It is lovingly moulded to the shape of the other two breasts.' In his female nudes, Ingres's imaginative sense of line is given full rein. The modelling of their forms is freed from the constraint of the curved lines, and they blossom in carnal splendour, just like the materials and costumes in his female portraits. Ingres's linear treatment has the power to transform a human body into pure plastic form. Gaétan Picon described it as 'catharsis of the erotic', and as such it is an important contribution to painting.

The preparatory drawings for the *Grande Odalisque* reveal the stages of this transformation. The first drawing is wholly realistic, and Ingres, who thinks in visual terms, transcribes literally what he sees. The succeeding studies mark his increasing distance from the object. He traces his drawings, refining the outline, just as in the portraits he imposes geometrical form into his monumental figures. This is the process which lies at the root of the archaicism, the expressionism, the 'Gothic' leanings, and the distortions for which he was criticized by his contemporaries. The body of the *Grande Odalisque* is contained only by this ideal curve, which has the purity of a Botticelli. She has neither 'bones, blood, life or relief.'

Line becomes an end in itself. Line alone creates form and movement, setting up purely plastic rhythms: true movement, on the other hand, is always that of volume. The subject is transposed into abstract equivalents of signs. In this sense, Ingres may be described as the creator of a plastic language which has been used by all modern painters since Matisse and Picasso. As in the work of Kandinsky, the line creates the plane, since the continuous curve circumscribes an area which becomes the entire space of the picture. The illusion of modelling has disappeared. The canvas is reduced to its two dimensions and is constructed by means of flattened planes of colour.

Ingres thus makes a definitive break with the vision of the Renaissance based on perspective, which is all the more remarkable in that Ingres was the least visionary or revolutionary of painters, and was regarded by his contemporaries as an incomprehensible anomaly. Landon wrote of the *Grande Odalisque*, 'The light is so evenly spread and distributed with such lack of skill that the colours of the flesh are dull and monotonous.'

The more perceptive critics, among them Baudelaire, could hardly fail to recognize the lyrical quality of the curved line. Indeed, in Ingres's flowing sense of line, inspired by the female form, lies the key to his lyricism. Baudelaire was the first to point out that the female form was the subject most ideally suited to Ingres's genius. 'He follows the subtle curves of their body with the devotion of a lover.' The lyrical line ceases to be dependent on the model, and is redolent of the sensations, the love, of the man observing her. In Ingres, this love is purely sensual. His nudes are quite unlike the forms in the work of Delacroix, which are transfigured by the drama of the subject. Ingres's starting point is always perception. Idealization is attained through a process of abstraction; Ingres' sensuality is filtered through his detachment.

Around the period 1817-19, Ingres discovered the theme of the Turkish Bath in the letters of Lady Mary Wortley-Montagu, from which he copied a passage on the baths at Hadrianople. His own theory of pure enjoyment applied easily to the fashionable orientalism of the period, which satisfied the more unreal elements in his fantasies. Ingres's Orient is no more real than the Orient of the Romantics: it is simply a vehicle for his eroticism. The *Small Bather* of 1828 (*pls 49-51*) is an early version of the Turkish Bath theme, and is a very unassuming harem compared to the opulent array of flesh in *The Turkish Bath*. The companions of the *Bather of Valpinçon* are based on prints belonging to Ingres which illustrate Oriental costume. He dispenses with these for *The Turkish Bath*: the creature which people the later composition are entirely his own creation. The *Odalisque with Slave* (*pls 62-65*), inspired by a Persian miniature, was painted in 1842, his second version of the subject. The odalisque is accompanied by a woman playing a musical instrument and a black male slave.

For the time being the Turkish Bath theme was put aside for other tasks. In 1843-48, Ingres was working on the *Golden Age* fresco. In this period his treatment of the human body was at its most imaginative and most fluid. The death of his wife interrupted his work on the fresco, to which he was never to return. In 1848 he painted the *Venus Anadyomene*, with its references to Botticelli, which recur though in a softer, less marked form, in *The Source* (*pl. 70*) in 1856, inspired by Jean Goujon's figures in the Fountain of the Innocents. His *Jupiter and Antiope* (*pls 66-67*) was painted in 1851.

Venus Anadyomene, 1848. Oil on canvas, 152.8×92 cm. Chantilly, Musée Condé.

The Turkish Bath was completed in 1859, and Napoleon III bought it in the same year. The picture then was not quite as we know it today: it was rectangular and without certain decorative details. In 1860 Ingres took back the painting in exchange for his *Self-portrait at the Age of Twenty-four*, making additions to it and giving it the shape of a Renaissance *tondo*, which freezes the enclosed space and heightens its quality of unreality.

It is this canvas, rather than the cold declamatory *Homer*, which is an apotheosis: an apotheosis of 'bodies content to be bodies'. The figure of the inexpressive woman, wholly absorbed in the opulence of her flesh, who appears so often in Ingres's work, even in the historical subjects, is repeated here many times over. The woman whose breast is caressed by a companion, is the same figure as the angel on the right in the *Vow of Louis XIII (pls 43-44)*, and as the angel who crowns Homer. The woman holding a cup in the background, to the left, has the solemn pose of the Odyssey. The standing dancer is in the inverted position of the *Source* and Angelica. The bather in the foreground, for which Ingres made an extraordinary preparatory study *(pl. 74)*, with different positions of the arms, so that the figure looks like a Hindu goddess, is a more lascivious version of the *Odalisque with Slave*. The *Grande Odalisque* has become a musician. Ingres's deep-rooted sensuality unfolds in this bold fantasy, where all the desired creatures of his imagination mingle in voluptuous confusion.

These images are 'transposed into an unrelated space' where perspective is merely mirage. The light does not mould the forms, nor is it even a steady light. It is reflected light. It is rather like the light in the *Bather of Valpinçon*, which spreads over the plane, and, rather than illuminating the canvas, seems to make the colour unreal. It gives the colours the 'Japanese' quality, which has often been remarked on in Ingres's work: colours without intensity, almost transparent, arranged not in contrast but in subtle harmony. In *The Turkish Bath*, this light isolates the group in the foreground, and their bodies seem to be irradiated by an inner glow. It is the light which breaks up the space in the canvas. The group bathed in light is wrenched out of the confused mass of bodies piled up against each other. The contrast of the two planes, the dark plane of the background and the brighter plane of the figures in the foreground, gives a false impression of depth. The illusion of perspective is heightened by the remarkable variation in the size of the figures from one plane to the other. The monumental figures of the illuminated group are in striking contrast to the miniature-like figures in the crowd in the background.

The planes are linked by the strange group made up of the black slave and the bather combing another woman's hair. This bather would be an androgynous figure, but for the exaggerated, thrust-forward shoulders which compensate for the flatness of her breast. The Negress is a Gauguinesque creation, a face with no visible body, whose massiveness groups her with the women in the foreground, while her dark colour draws her into the background. The thematic importance of this transitional group is questionable. They are rather like the prone figures in Renaissance paintings, whose function, like knives in a still-life, is to give an impression of depth. They have a disturbing, sensual quality. The impression of bodies clustered together is rendered by a linear rhythm which contains and freezes them. The curves of the bodies weave a baroque tangle, which has to be balanced by the solemn figures in a vertical rhythm taken from the musician in the foreground. The structure of the composition makes the figures, arranged in a single spatial dimension, insubstantial. The line enclosing the female bodies no longer has the taut, fine Botticellian elegance of the *Bather of Valpinçon*. In spite of the sensuously abundant flesh, Ingres distorts the figures giving them an air of unreality. Look, for example, at the back, bent at right angles, of the woman being caressed by her neighbour.

These women 'immured in their corporeality' have the narcissism of goddesses. They are indifferent to being gazed at or touched. Vain bodies, the untouchable objects of desire or dreams, their caresses have the detachment of ritual gestures. Just as his historical paintings stand back from the event they depict, Ingres's *Turkish Bath* is not a drama of the flesh, but a ceremony. It is a true 'catharsis

31

of the erotic'. Desire takes the form of visual ceremony, and these daughters of desire become objects of contemplation.

In 1905 *The Turkish Bath* was the revelation of the Salon d'Automne, and Ingres's work made a deep impression on those artists who were to revolutionize art in the twentieth century. In the nineteenth century, Ingres had influenced his pupils, mediocre neoclassicists, who could almost be described as French Pre-Raphaelites. Their aim was to revive mural painting, to which Ingres's style, and his method of building a composition with successive layers, was highly applicable, even though his larger canvases were not his most successful works. These fresco painters, Hippolyte and Paul Flandrin, Mottez, Ziegler, Amaury-Duval, Orsel, Janmot and Chenavard, flooded the churches of Lyons and Paris. The most gifted of these disciples was Chassériau, who achieved new and happy results with his nudes in the manner of Ingres. His women, with their languid curves, are absorbed by their own secret world of fantasy. Chassériau was an equally gifted decorator, and Puvis de Chavannes was to be influenced by his frescoes in the Cour des Comptes.

At the end of the nineteenth century, Ingres was to be the spiritual master of Puvis and the Symbolists, who were reacting against the dissolution of form wrought by the Impressionists. They believed in the idealization of line. Without going into the complexities of their aesthetic principles here, Ingres was for them the artist who had seen painting as a system of plastic transcription. All those painters who tended to intellectualize art were to acknowledge Ingres as a precursor. Even Renoir was to go through an Ingres phase before rediscovering his sense of form.

The work of Ingres was one of the main sources of figurative art in the twentieth century for two complementary reasons. He abandoned the Renaissance system of perspective, and the conventions which link it to the subject. He is an artist who paints as he sees, who 'constructs sensations', as Cézanne was to try to do. The role played by Ingres is analogous to that of Cézanne, but Ingres lacked a clear understanding of the problems raised in his own painting. The Post-Impressionists were to follow Ingres's lead: Gauguin with his emphatic drawing and large chromatic planes; and the draughtsmen, Toulouse-Lautrec and Degas, made use not only of line but of layout and detached perspective. Degas was a great admirer of Ingres, and possessed nineteen of his paintings and thirty-three drawings. Seurat, too, was influenced by Ingres, and at the age of twenty-four did some drawings based on *The Source*, and later copied *Angelica*.

Ingres, who had substituted architectural construction of the picture for illusionist realism, was also recognized as a forerunner by the Cubists, among them La Fresnaye, and above all by Picasso. Ingres's influence formed an element of continuity between the different periods in Picasso's career. There is the debt to Ingres in the archaism of the drawings in his early life. In his Cubist period he made the final break, begun by Ingres, with the perspectival vision of the Renaissance. Picasso's ' classical ' period bears traces of Ingres's monumental geometry, and Ingres had also shown the way to his later expressionist distortion.

Ingres, who believed in the power of seeing, and who was concerned solely with tangible appearances which he translated into painting, bears a certain responsibility for the indifference of the artist towards his subject, and eventually for its abandonment. He is the forerunner of pure painting, from abstract art to the most rigid formalism. Ingres's great achievement was to have treated painting as a system, a plastic language governed by its own rules of line and colour. In this sense, since our vision has been so drastically altered by the artists of the early twentieth century, no painter conscious of plastic problems has been untouched by the influence of Ingres. When Maurice Denis said that, before a painting is a successful work of art, it is a flat surface with colours arranged in a particular order, he was referring to the teachings of Ingres. Bissière is also following on from Ingres when he makes his corollary to Denis's thesis. He says that there are no dead surfaces in a painting; everything is painted. ' A painting is a surface in which the most distant planes are brought violently forward in order to give the whole the maximum expressive impact, with methods which belong to painting alone.'

The artist who has given the most complete expression to the teachings of Ingres is undoubtedly Matisse. Like Ingres, he brings shapes to the surface by means of colour, using line to give them rhythm. The affinity between the two men is perhaps something more than conformity to the same figurative approach. Matisse takes the same sensual delight in vision, developing it more freely and with happier results.

What part does Ingres's influence play in the avant-garde movement of today, which is a reaction against 'pure' painting and against painting itself? Perhaps this marks Ingres's limit, revealed whenever, either in his own painting, or the painting that was to follow him, the visual element in reality or in the painting is abandoned.

Once again, the paradoxical nature of Ingres's personality prevents us from making any rigid or definitive judgment of his work. His portrayal of women is conditioned by his sensual imagination, which the Surrealists have praised as his 'alienated' eroticism; and it is still too soon to assess the importance of his influence on present-day art. Ingres remains a controversial artist, and even if his role in artistic development is now less significant, his vitality is too great to allow us as yet to assign him a definitive place among the artists of the past.

Ingres and the Critics

The basic critical texts on Ingres are still the following, in spite of their age: Henri Delaborde, *Ingres, sa vie ses travaux, sa doctrine ...*, Paris 1870; Henry Lapauze, *Ingres, sa vie et son œuvre*, Paris 1911.

Monographs and specialist studies: Jean Alazard, *Ingres et l'ingrisme*, Paris 1950; Jean Cassou, *Ingres*, Brussels 1947; Raymond Cogniat, *Ingres, écrits sur l'art*, Paris 1947; Pierre Courthion, *Ingres raconté par lui-même et par ses amis,* Geneva 1947-48; Waldemar George, *Dessins d'Ingres*, Paris 1967; Ingres, essays IX and X in Lapauze, 1911; Alexandrine Miller, ' Ingres, three methods of drawing as revealed by his crayon portraits ', in *Art in America*, West Point, January 1938; Hans Naef ' Travaux de Hans Naef sur Ingres, 1946-66 ' (Bibliography), *B.M.I.*, Montauban, July 1966; Hans Naef, *Rome vue par Ingres*, Lausanne 1960; Gaetan Picon, *Ingres*, Geneva 1967; Robert Rosenblum, *Ingres*, London and New York 1967; Norman Schlenoff, *Ingres, ses sources littéraires*, Paris 1956; Jean Lacambre and Daniel Ternois, *Ingres et son temps*, Paris 1967 (catalogue of exhibition, Montauban, 1967); Thiebault-Sisson, ' Le paysage dans l'œuvre de Ingres ', in *La Renaissance*, May 1927; Georges Wildenstein, *Ingres*, London 1954 (catalogue); *Ingres*, Catalogue of centenary exhibition, Paris 1957.

Madame Destouche. Pencil drawing, 43×28.5 cm. Paris, Musée du Louvre.

36

Notes on the plates

1 Self-portrait at the Age of Twenty-four, 1804. Oil on canvas, 78×61 cm. Chantilly, Musée Condé.

2 M. Philibert Rivière, 1805. Oil on canvas, 116×89 cm. Paris, Louvre.

3 Mme Philibert Rivière, 1805. Oil on canvas, 116×82 cm. Paris, Louvre.

4-5 Mlle Rivière, 1805. Oil on canvas, 100×70 cm. Paris, Louvre.

6-7 Mme Aymon (La Belle Zélie), 1806. Oil on canvas, 59×49 cm. Rouen, Musée des Beaux-Arts.

8-9 View of the Villa Medici, 1806. Oil on panel, diameter 16 cm. Montauban, Musée Ingres.

10-11 View of the Villa Borghese, 1806. Oil on panel, diameter 16 cm. Montauban, Musée Ingres.

12-13 The Casino of Raphael in Rome, 1806-07. Oil on panel, diameter 16 cm. Paris, Musée des Arts Décoratifs.

14 François-Marius Granet, c. 1807. Oil on canvas, 72×61 cm. Aix-en-Provence, Musée Granet.

15-16 Mme Devauçay, 1807. Oil on canvas, 76×59 cm. Chantilly, Musée Condé.

17-18 Oedipus and the Sphinx, 1808. Oil on canvas, 189×144 cm. Paris, Louvre.

19-20 Bather of Valpinçon, 1808. Oil on canvas, 146×97 cm. Paris, Louvre.

21 View of Tivoli, 1808-10. Graphite and sepia, 18.7×27 cm. Montauban, Musée Ingres.

22 Jean-Baptiste Desdéban, c. 1810. Oil on canvas, 63×49 cm. Besaçon, Musée des Beaux-Arts.

23 Jupiter and Thetis, 1811. Oil on canvas, 327×260 cm. Aix-en-Provence, Musée Granet.

24 M. Pierre-Louis-Antoine Cordier, 1811. Detail. Oil on canvas, 90×70 overall. Paris, Louvre.

25-27 Romulus, Conqueror of Acron, brings back the Spolia Opima, 1812. Oil on canvas, 276×530 cm. Paris, Ecole des Beaux-Arts.

28 The Dream of Ossian, 1812-13. Oil on canvas, 348×275 cm. Montauban, Musée Ingres.

29-32 Grande Odalisque, 1814. Oil on canvas, 91×162 cm. Paris, Louvre.

33 Mme de Senonnes, 1814-16. Oil on canvas, 106×84 cm. Nantes, Musée des Beaux-Arts.

34 Study for ' Roger and Angelica ', 1819. Oil on canvas, 84.5×42.5 cm. Paris, Louvre.

35-38 Roger and Angelica, 1819. Oil on canvas, 147×190 cm. Paris, Louvre.

39 Paolo and Francesca, 1819. Oil on canvas, 48×39 cm. Angers, Musée des Beaux-Arts.

40 Don Pedro de Toledo kisses the Sword of Henry IV, 1820. Oil on panel, 48×40 cm. Oslo, private collection.

41 The Sistine Chapel, 1820. Oil on canvas, 69×55 cm. Paris, Louvre.

42 Count Nicolas Dmitriévitch de Gouriev, 1821. Oil on canvas, 107×86 cm. Leningrad, State Hermitage Museum.

43-44 The Vow of Louis XIII, 1824. Oil on canvas, 421×262 cm. Montauban, Cathédrale Notre-Dame.

45-47 Mme Marcotte de Sainte-Marie, 1826. Oil on canvas, 93×74 cm. Paris, Louvre.

48 The Odyssey, c. 1827. Oil on canvas applied to panel, 61×55 cm. Lyons, Musée des Beaux-Arts. This is a study for the *Apotheosis of Homer* (1827), in which painting the Odyssey is shown seated to the right at the feet of Homer enthroned.

49-51 The Small Bather (Interior of a Harem), 1828. Oil on canvas, 35×27 cm. Paris, Louvre.

52 M. Louis-François Bertin, 1832. Oil on canvas, 116×95 cm. Paris, Louvre.

53-54 Martyrdom of St Symphorian, 1834. Oil on canvas, 407×339 cm. Autun, Cathédrale Saint-Lazare.

55-56 Raphael and the Fornarina, 1840. Oil on canvas, 35×27 cm. Columbus, Ohio, Gallery of Fine Arts.

57 Charity, 1842. Oil on canvas, diameter 110 cm. Paris, Louvre (reserve collection). Cartoon for window in chapel of St Ferdinand.

58 St Adelaide, 1842. Detail. Oil on canvas, 210×92 cm. overall. Paris, Louvre (reserve collection). Cartoon for window in chapel of St Ferdinand.

59-60 Cherubini and the Muse of Lyric Poetry, 1842. Oil on canvas, 105×94 cm. Paris, Louvre.

61 Fernand Philippe, Duke of Orleans, 1842. Oil on canvas, 158×122 cm. Louveciennes, Comte de Paris collection.

62-65 Odalisque with Slave, 1842. Oil on canvas, 76×105 cm. Baltimore, Md., Museum of Art.

66-67 Jupiter and Antiope, 1851. Oil on canvas, 32×43 cm. Paris, Louvre.

68 Joan of Arc at the Coronation of Charles VII, 1854. Oil on canvas, 240×178 cm. Paris, Louvre.

69 Virgin of the Host, 1854. Oil on canvas, diameter 113 cm. Paris, Louvre.

70 The Source, 1856. Oil on canvas, 164×82 cm. Paris, Louvre.

71-72 Mme Moitessier, 1856. Oil on canvas, 120×92 cm. Paris, Louvre.

73 Self-portrait, 1858. Oil on canvas, 64×54 cm. Florence, Uffizi.

74 Study for 'The Turkish Bath', 1862. Oil on card, 25×26 cm. Montauban, Musée Ingres.

75-78 The Turkish Bath, 1862. Oil on canvas applied to panel, diameter 108 cm. Paris, Louvre.

79 Study for 'Jesus among the Doctors', 1862. Oil on canvas, patches, overall 59×45 cm. Montauban, Musée Ingres.

80-82 Jesus among the Doctors, 1862. Oil on canvas, 265×320 cm. Montauban, Musée Ingres.

83-84 Antiochus and Stratonice, 1866. Oil on canvas, 61×92 cm. Montpellier, Musée Fabre.

1

10

11

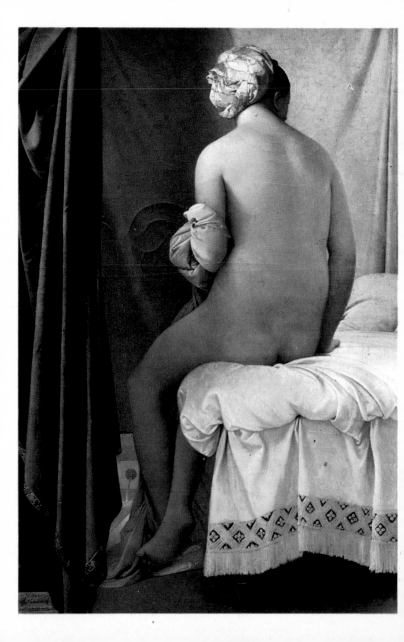

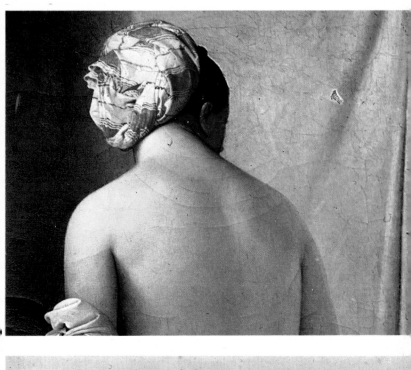

VIRG. DEIP.
REGN. VOV
LUDOV. XIII
A. R. S. H.
CIↃIↃCXXXVIII
FEB.

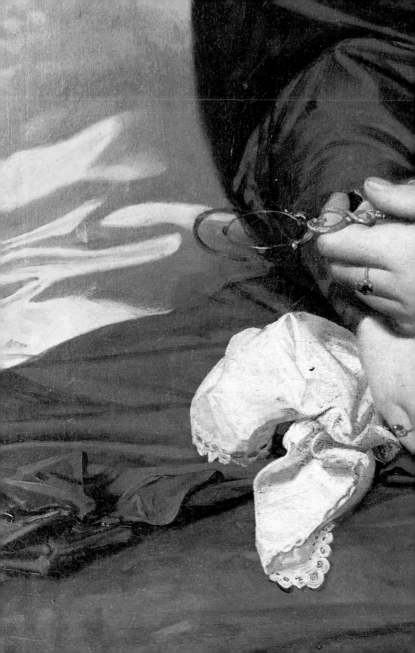

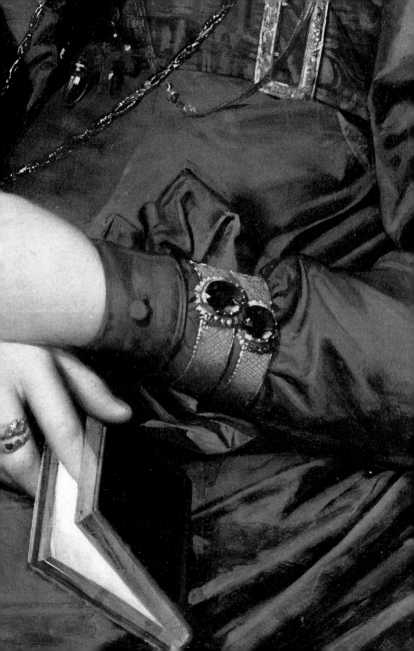

ΟΛΥΣΣΕΙΑ

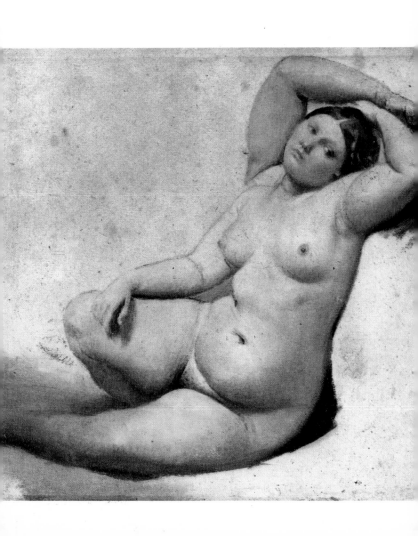

ÆTATIS LXXXII

82